Many years ago,
when my people were happier than they are now,
they used to celebrate the Festival of Flowers in the spring . . .
All the girls who have flower-names dance along together . . .
Each one gathers the flower she is named for,
and then all weave them into wreaths and crowns . . .
each girl in turn singing of herself . . .

I, Sarah Winnemucca, am a shell-flower.
My name is Thocmetony.

PAIUTE PRINCESS
THE STORY OF SARAH WINNEMUCCA

DEBORAH KOGAN RAY

FRANCES FOSTER BOOKS
FARRAR STRAUS GIROUX
NEW YORK

A well-dressed audience of fifteen hundred people packed into historic Christ Church in Philadelphia in October 1883. Half an hour before the speaker was scheduled to arrive, every seat was taken, and the aisles were full.

The person they awaited had met with presidents and delivered hundreds of lectures across the country. She was known to be an eloquent speaker and a fiery advocate for her people. Her book, *Life Among the Piutes: Their Wrongs and Claims*, had been published that year. It was the first autobiography written by a Native American woman.

Newspapers had dubbed her "Princess Sarah."

The audience burst into applause as Sarah Winnemucca strode onstage and began the story of her remarkable journey.

I was a very small child when the first white people came into our country. They came like a lion, yes, like a roaring lion . . . and I have never forgotten their first coming.

My people were scattered at that time over nearly all the territory now known as Nevada. My grandfather was chief of the entire Piute nation.

Sarah was named Thocmetony, which means shellflower, when she was born in about 1844.

For generation after generation, her people had lived peacefully in their harsh desert country, where, divided into bands, families roamed in search of food. For a short time, little Thocmetony would know the traditional life that revolved around the seasons.

Her father, Winnemucca, the antelope charmer of their band—the Kuyuidika-a—led the springtime hunt across the vast sagebrush-dotted plains. In the summer, her mother, Tuboitony, and the other women gathered wild grains along the Humboldt River, where fishing was bountiful. Young and old made the autumn pilgrimage to the mountains, where the piñon trees grew, to harvest pine nuts.

Thocmetony's grandfather Chief Truckee welcomed the arrival of white people to their land, for, according to legend, they were the banished children of the tribe. He believed that befriending them would heal old wounds.

"I want to love them as I love all of you," he told his people, and he made them promise to always keep the peace.

In 1845, he befriended explorer John Charles Frémont, and joined his California-bound expedition as a guide, staying on in California to serve with Frémont's army during the Bear Flag Revolt against Mexican rule in 1846.

Thocmetony's grandfather returned with stories of the marvels he had seen in the white man's world, and carried with him a letter of introduction written by Frémont that asked all who met "Captain Truckee" to treat him well. He called this letter his "rag friend."

To Truckee, written words were the source of the white man's power.

"Our white brothers are a mighty nation . . . This can talk to all our white brothers, and our white sisters, and their children," he told Thocmetony.

Very late that fall, my grandfather and my father and a great many more went down to the Humboldt River to fish . . . When they came back . . . they said there were some white people living at the Humboldt sink . . . During the winter my people helped them. They gave them such as they had to eat.

There was no game to hunt when the desert lay blanketed in snow. Sharing their meager stores of nuts and grains was a sacrifice for Thocmetony's people.

They got a bitter repayment for their kindness.

That spring, a group of white men attacked a Kuyuidika-a fishing party camped along the river. Soon, fearful news arrived from other Paiute bands telling of more armed attacks by white men, along with horrific tales of the ill-fated Donner party, emigrants who had resorted to eating members of their own group when their wagon train was stranded in the high Sierras.

Hair-raising accounts of the brutal misdeeds were told and retold around the campfire. The ancient myth of the cannibal owl—a monster that devoured small children—merged into the telling of the bloodcurdling story.

Oh, what a fright we all got one morning to hear some white people were coming . . . My poor mother was carrying my little sister on her back, and trying to make me run; but I was so frightened I could not move my feet . . . My aunt overtook us, and she said to my mother: "Let us bury our girls, or we shall all be killed and eaten up." So they went to work and buried us, and told us if we heard any noise not to cry out . . . {They} planted sage bushes over our faces to keep the sun from burning them . . . With my heart throbbing, and not daring to breathe, we lay there all day. It seemed that the night would never come.

At last Thocmetony heard whispering. Afraid to make a sound, she lay stone-still as footsteps drew closer. Then she heard her mother's voice calling.

Soon she was safe in her mother's arms.

But her terror did not go away.

When her grandfather decided that his sons and daughters and their children should accompany him to California to learn about the white man's world, she was certain that terrible danger lay ahead.

How I did cry, and wished that I had staid at home with my father!

Her grandfather's assurances that his rag friend would keep them safe, and that white people were not the evil cannibal owls in her nightmares, did nothing to calm her.

She hid inside her mother's rabbit skin robes, sobbing, as her grandfather led them along the Carson River toward the towering Sierras.

At last we came to a very large encampment of white people . . . My grandfather called me to him, and said I must not be afraid of the white people, for they are very good . . .

When they were coming nearer . . . I peeped round my mother to see them . . . They were the first ones I had ever seen in my life.

Dread of an unknown menace vanished. Tears were replaced by wonder, as Thocmetony witnessed the power of her grandfather's "talking" rag friend.

After Chief Truckee's white brothers looked at the paper, there were handshakes of friendship. Sacks of flour and other provisions were offered, as well as clothing for the men and women of his family.

Friendly encounters continued on the heavily used emigrant trail. But when sweet treats were handed out to the Paiute children, Thocmetony hung back from the others, still wary of close contact with the white strangers.

Only when she became deathly ill from touching a plant called poison oak, and a gentle woman brought medicine and nursed her back to health, did she learn that a white person could be kind and caring, and trusted.

Through her fever, she heard the woman's comforting voice softly murmuring over and over, "Poor little girl, it is too bad!"

They were the first English words Thocmetony learned.

I kept thinking over what {Grandpa} said to me about the good white people, and saying to myself, "I will make friends with them when we come into California."

It became dark before we got to the town, but we could see something like stars away ahead of us.

The town of Stockton, aglow in the night sky, held Thocmetony spellbound.

A hub for fortune-seeking forty-niners, Stockton had grown into a bustling settlement of thousands in the two years since gold was discovered in California at Sutter's Mill in 1848. Pack mules and oxcarts plied the docks. Steamboat bells chimed from the river. Never had Thocmetony seen so many people in one place—more than she imagined existed.

The white man's world did hold marvels!

She would soon learn that it also held perils.

Life at a ranch along the San Joaquin River, where her grandfather's friend Hiram Scott ran an inn and ferry service, began with trouble. When the men of Thocmetony's family were hired as vaqueros to take herds of horses to graze in the Sierra foothills, the women and children were left behind. Camped at the river, they became prey for the rough-and-tumble ferry crews.

The men . . . would come into our camp and ask my mother to give our sister to them. They would come in at night, and we would all scream and cry; but that would not stop them.

When Hiram Scott learned of this, he swiftly moved the women and children indoors, where he could protect them.

The first night that Thocmetony slept in a room she felt imprisoned. But she quickly adapted to the house. The way white people lived fascinated the curious six-year-old.

Her fingers itched to touch the thin dishes from which they ate their meals at a "high thing"—what she called a table. The red plush dining chairs were so enchanting that she sat on them whenever no one was looking.

By late spring, when the family prepared to return to their homeland, she was happily repeating the new English words she had learned from Hiram Scott. Among them was the name he called her—Sarah.

Now, there were a great many of our white brothers everywhere through our country, and mines or farms here and there.

The white man had come to stay, and with him came diseases never known among the Paiute. Cholera had already killed many of the tribe.

Fearful of contact with the settlers, Winnemucca and many of the Kuyuidika-a band moved to more distant tribal lands.

Sarah became a child of two worlds—following the traditional ways when living with her parents, but not when accompanying her grandfather for long visits to California, where she lived with his white friends. English and Spanish were spoken in the towns and on the ranches, and Sarah's ear for language was acute. By the time she was ten years old she spoke both languages well.

Impressed by her quickness at learning, her grandfather hoped that someday she would guide their people in a changing world. In 1857, he arranged for Sarah's "adoption" by the Ormsbys, a family that lived in Nevada, along the Carson River, in a town called Genoa. In exchange for doing household chores and being a companion for their only child, nine-year-old Lizzie Jane, Sarah was allowed to sit in on the lessons that Margaret Ormsby gave her daughter.

It was a happy and exciting time for Sarah.

With each new letter she learned to shape and each new word she recognized, she became determined to learn more. What joy her beloved grandpa would get when she could read and write "rag friends" for him!

Borrowing books from the family's library, she stayed up late into the night, sounding out each word and practicing script.

Major William Ormsby, a former military man, was a leading figure in the growing town, owning several stores and the stagecoach stop for the Carson Valley Express. Sarah got to know all the townspeople, and the miners who worked gold claims in nearby Johntown and Gold Hill, and she met many travelers.

The once-fearful child, who had cowered at the thought of seeing a white person, now fully embraced their language and customs. Dressed in fashionable clothes, with her long hair curled *taibo* (white-person) style, the lively fourteen-year-old was a popular partner at the Saturday night square dances.

During her year and a half with the Ormsbys, Sarah was treated well, and she developed great affection for the family. But prejudice existed among all the settlers—even the Ormsbys. They were quick to believe the worst of native people when two white shopkeepers were found shot to death. Three men of the Washoe tribe were swiftly arrested. Their families pleaded that they were with them when the crime occurred, but no one would listen.

I ran to Mrs. Ormsby crying. I thought my poor heart would break. I said to her, "I believe those Washoe women. They say their men are all innocent."

The men were killed. Later, it was discovered that the real murderers were white bandits.

In June of 1859, news from the eastern slopes of the Sierra Nevada made banner headlines across the nation. A miner named Henry Comstock discovered silver.

The legendary Comstock Lode would turn out to be one of the greatest mineral strikes in history. It triggered an immediate mining stampede.

They came like a lion, yes, like a roaring lion.

Within weeks, thousands arrived from the nearby California goldfields and from distant places. The boomtown of Virginia City sprang up. In their quest for sudden wealth, miners overran the Paiute hunting lands and recklessly chopped down the piñon trees for mine supports.

Winter that year was unusually long and bitter. Many Paiute froze to death. Others starved. Desperate and angry, bands camped outside Virginia City, eating the white man's garbage. Talk of war against the invaders began.

Sarah's father and aged grandfather pleaded with their people to keep the peace. So did her cousin Numaga, known for his bravery. As the tribe's designated war chief, he eloquently argued in council against going into battle.

"Your enemies are like the sands in the bed of your rivers; when taken away they only give place for more to come and settle there . . . They will come like the sand in a whirlwind and drive you from your homes. You will be forced among the barren rocks of the north, where your ponies will die; where you will see the women and old men starve, and listen to the cries of your children for food."

Sadly, every word he said would come true.

The bloody battles of the Pyramid Lake War of 1860 ended in defeat for the Paiute. Before the year was over, the United States Army had built Fort Churchill on the Carson River, and many of the tribe had been moved onto a reservation at Pyramid Lake.

We could see the signal-fires of death on every mountain-top . . . Our people gathered from far and near, for my poor, poor grandpa was going very fast . . .

I crept up to him. I could hardly believe he would never speak to me again. I knelt beside him, and took his dear old face in my hands, and looked at him quite a while. I could not speak. I felt the world growing cold; everything seemed dark. The great light had gone out . . . I was only a simple child, yet I knew what a great man he was . . . I knew how necessary it was for our good that he should live.

Though the peace that Sarah's grandfather had worked so hard to keep had been broken, both Paiute and settlers joined together. His many white friends erected a cross on which his name was carved. As he had requested, his people placed his rag friend over his heart.

Such a scene I never had seen before. Everybody would take his dead body in their arms and weep. Poor papa kept his body two days.

In Paiute custom, he was buried with all his earthly possessions—clothing, bows and arrows, smoking pipes—and his hut was burned. As a sign of great respect, six horses were killed and sacrificed.

Winnemucca, who would now be leader, spoke over Truckee's grave: "A good man is gone. The white man knows he was good, for he guided him round deserts and led him in paths where there was grass and good water. His people know he was good, for he loved them and cared for them and came home to them to die."

Sarah's beloved grandfather had been a bold adventurer, a seeker of peace and learning, unafraid to step into a world others feared. Through her tears, Sarah vowed that she would follow the path her grandfather had set.

My sister and I were taken to San Jose, California. Brother Natchez and five other men went with us. On our arrival we were placed in the "Sisters' School."

Her grandfather's last request before he died was that Sarah and her little sister Elma be taken to Hiram Scott, who had promised to place them in a school run by nuns.

Sarah's grandfather had befriended the Sisters of Notre Dame de Namur, who were members of a French order, when they first arrived in California in 1851 to set up a school. From humble beginnings, and with a mission to provide education for all girls—whether poor or rich—the school had grown and prospered. With prosperity came change.

The Academy of Notre Dame, its ornate buildings set among flowering gardens, was now a prestigious school attended by the daughters of the wealthy, where girls were taught all the classical subjects, as well as fine sewing and genteel manners.

To sixteen-year-old Sarah, entering this alien world was like stepping into a dream. She threw herself into her classes in history, geography, and writing and immersed herself in reading stories. She learned to create delicate silk stitchery, to speak with perfect diction, and to ride sidesaddle like a lady.

But the dream soon ended. After a flood of complaints from parents about "dirty savages" attending school with their children, Sarah and her sister were sent home.

Hurt and angry, Sarah cried the whole way back to Nevada on the long stagecoach ride.

It was the last time she would attend a school, but her short experience had given her skills that she would later use. She tried to imagine how different the world would be if Paiute children could go to a school where they were loved and welcomed.

Sarah returned to a world that was once more changing.

In addition to the thousands of miners and settlers, workers had arrived to survey Paiute tribal land for the railroad that would cross the country.

This reservation, given in 1860, was at first sixty miles long and fifteen wide . . . No white people lived there at the time it was given us.

Year by year, the land at Pyramid Lake set aside for the Paiute was grabbed and claimed by white people. The mouth of the Truckee River, which was rich with fish, was taken over by the railroad. Ranchers herded their cattle into the valleys, where they consumed the wild grasses needed by the tribe for food.

By the fall of 1864, another starvation winter loomed ahead. Out of desperation, Sarah hatched a plan to bring attention to the tribe's plight. From years of living among white people, she knew that despite their prejudice, they were fascinated by Indian ceremony of any kind.

Chief Winnemucca, along with Sarah, Elma, Natchez, and a band of warriors—all in ceremonial garb—created a stir when they paraded through the streets of Virginia City. The parade halted in front of the stately International Hotel, where Chief Winnemucca gave a speech about his people's need for money to buy food and blankets, which Sarah translated for the assembled crowd. Then they passed a hat for donations.

Sarah was right. The free-spending miners loved Indian spectacle.

It was the first of many increasingly dramatic events staged by "Princess Sarah." Though her action-packed skits, like the Grand Scalp Dance, bore no resemblance to the way her people really lived, they were what white audiences craved, and they drew the crowds for her father's speeches. The performances packed theaters from Virginia City to San Francisco.

But at the end of their tour, after paying expenses, the Winnemucca family returned to Pyramid Lake discouraged and nearly empty-handed.

It was early in the spring . . . when a company of soldiers came through . . . and stopped and spoke to some of my people . . . They said . . . that they would kill everything that came in their way.

Many Paiute, having lost their own land, now lived in enclaves near the towns throughout the Comstock, eking out an existence working for the white settlers. The men cut and sold firewood. The women served as maids and cooks. Sarah was working as a seamstress in the mining town of Dayton when trouble for her people began anew. Though whites held the power, many lived in dread of Indian attacks—minor incidents fed their fears and inflamed their anger. Cries to "let loose the dogs of war" erupted when three hungry Paiute stole some cattle.

Newly appointed Captain Almond B. Wells, eager to make a reputation as an "Indian fighter," was dispatched with a troop from Fort Churchill and went in hot pursuit.

Unaware of the theft or of their own imminent peril, a group of the Kuyuidika-a band was camped at Mud Lake, east of the reservation. Chief Winnemucca and the men had gone in search of antelope. Only the women, children, and old men remained.

Before dawn on March 14, 1865, Wells staged a surprise attack.

The soldiers rode up to their encampment and fired into it . . . After the soldiers had killed all but some little children and babies still tied up in their baskets, the soldiers took them also, and set the camp on fire and threw them into the flames to see them burn alive. I had one baby brother killed there.

Wells and the soldiers who took part in the Mud Lake massacre went unpunished. But Winnemucca, who had never harmed a person, was declared a dangerous renegade when he sought isolation from a world that had caused him so much pain and fled north with members of the band to the remote Steens Mountain.

Sarah would take a different path. Her pain would lead her to fight for justice for her people.

This is the way all the Indian agents get rich. The first thing they do is to start a store; the next thing is to take in cattle men, and cattle men pay the agent one dollar a head. In this way they get rich very soon, so that they can have their gold-headed canes, with their names engraved on them.

Since its creation, the Pyramid Lake Reservation had been run by a succession of greedy, unscrupulous agents. The men hired by the Bureau of Indian Affairs (BIA) took bribes from big companies and ranchers. Desperately needed food and clothing sent by the government for distribution to the Paiute were instead sold off to the settlers for profit.

Sarah's first battle was to take on the corruption and abuse. She was not only fluent in English—she also had a sharp tongue. And she was not afraid to use it, whether she was face-to-face with an agent or giving interviews to newspaper reporters.

She also possessed skills that no other Paiute on the reservation had. She could read and write. She wrote letters to government officials, to newspapers, and to the Army. When she had no ink, she wrote in fish blood.

A letter written to the Army about a dispute finally got results. After seeing Sarah's people at Pyramid Lake near starvation, Captain Aaron Jerome denounced the agent and sent for three wagonloads of provisions from Fort Churchill. The young officer's act of compassion gained him Sarah's trust.

Sarah's greatest fear since her father's disappearance into the wilderness was that he would be killed by one of the many volunteer militias that hunted renegades for a reward. When Jerome offered shelter and protection for Chief Winnemucca at Camp McDermit—an Army post on the Oregon border—Sarah and her brother Natchez agreed to accompany him there.

"If you will give me your heart and hand, I will go and try to get my father to come to you," she promised.

Sarah's joy knew no bounds when Natchez led their weary father and his band into safety. Her life had already taken an unexpected turn. The post commander had hired her to act as interpreter for the Army.

Some of the interpreters are very ignorant, and don't understand English enough to know all that is said. This often makes trouble.

Sarah was perfect for the role of interpreter. Besides her language skills, she understood the two cultures and their customs.

Her accurate translation averted many misunderstandings, but it was difficult for her to remain neutral, as her job required, when she was aware of injustice.

She leaped at the chance to state her mind when Major Henry Douglas, the newly appointed superintendent of Indian Affairs for Nevada, asked for a written report on the reservation system from the Paiute point of view. Her account, detailing both grievances and suggestions for improvement, impressed him. He forwarded it to the federal offices in Washington, D.C., where it was passed around in official circles.

In May of 1870, Sarah's eloquent account was published in *Harper's Weekly*. Some readers of the well-known magazine could not believe a native woman wrote it. Others doubted that she really existed! But for many who read her powerful words, Sarah emerged as the voice of her people.

"If this is the kind of civilization awaiting us on the reserves, God grant that we may never be compelled to go on one," she had written.

She acknowledged the fair treatment received from the Army, but the future troubled her. Rumors were already flying that Camp McDermit would be closed as a refuge as soon as a new reservation, to be run by the Bureau of Indian Affairs, was completed in Oregon.

When the huge Malheur Reservation was opened in 1872, all the Paiute bands living in the region were urged to move there. With great trepidation, fearing that the BIA agent would be like all the others she had known, Sarah accepted the job of interpreter in April 1875.

I cannot tell or express how happy we were!

Samuel B. Parrish was unlike any agent Sarah and her people had encountered. The son of an abolitionist minister, he had grown up on the Oregon frontier believing all people were equal. At his first meeting with the tribe, he outlined a plan to make them self-sustaining through farming, education, and learning trades.

"The reservation is all yours," he told them. "The government has given it all to you and your children." On another occasion he said, "I will do all I can while I am with you."

He promised that all crops raised would belong to the people, that everyone would be fairly paid for their labor on the reservation, and that a school would be built for the children.

Though most tribal members had never farmed, they took on the tasks with enthusiasm—from the oldest to the youngest member. They tilled the soil and planted 120 acres with potatoes, green vegetables, and grains. By their first harvest celebration, several Paiute men had learned carpentry, and by spring the schoolhouse was finished. Sam Parrish's gentle sister-in-law Annie was to be the teacher, and Sarah her assistant.

On the first of May Mrs. Parrish and I opened the school. She had her organ at the schoolhouse, and played and sang songs . . . We had three hundred and five boys, twenty-three young men, sixty-nine girls, and nineteen young women. They learned very fast, and were glad to come to school . . . Mrs. Parrish . . . was very kind to the children. We all called her our white lily mother.

Most of the children spoke no English, and Sarah delighted in teaching them new words. She was a wonderful teacher, both patient and caring, and the students loved her. Never had she been more content. But like Sarah's own short formal education, her dream of school for her people would end too soon.

Local ranchers wanted to graze their livestock on the enormous reservation lands and complained to the Bureau of Indian Affairs that Parrish was treating the Paiute too well. Soon after, Samuel B. Parrish was fired.

On the twenty-eighth of June, 1876, our new agent, Major Rinehart, arrived . . . The agent said, "When I tell you to do anything I don't want any of you to dictate to me, but to go and do it" . . . All the time he was talking, my people hung their heads.

Sarah and the new agent soon became enemies.

William V. Rinehart, a former militia volunteer, prided himself on the number of "savages" he had killed. A cruel man of violent temper, he quickly put an end to Parrish's programs, withheld provisions, and beat tribal members—even small children. He was an ally of the ranchers, and he made it clear that he would be happy if the Paiute left Malheur, so that he could lease the land.

"If you don't like the way I do, you can all leave here," he spat out when Sarah protested his actions.

She repeatedly petitioned the Bureau of Indian Affairs about his crimes. Time after time they rebuffed her pleas. But that did not stop her protests. She wrote to magazines and gave interviews to newspapers condemning Rinehart. In turn he tried to ruin Sarah's reputation with public accusations that she was "a notorious liar and malicious schemer."

Tensions were exploding at Malheur under Rinehart's dictatorial rule. The peaceful Paiute were being turned onto the path to war. In the spring of 1878, the Bannock—a tribe that lived in the region—convinced several Paiute bands to join them in an uprising. When Chief Winnemucca, as head of the Kuyuidika-a band, pleaded for peace, he and his supporters were taken prisoner and held in the Bannock camp.

In desperation, Sarah turned to General Oliver O. Howard, who was in charge of fighting the Bannocks. She volunteered to be both interpreter and scout for the Army for the duration of the war. In return, Sarah wanted protection for her people—if she could free them.

Sarah was warned that she would have to cross over some of the roughest terrain in the West, most of it held by the hostile Bannocks. The chances of her survival were slim.

"There is nothing that will stop me," she declared, leaping on her horse.

Oh, such a sight my eyes met! . . . About three hundred and twenty-seven lodges, and about four hundred and fifty warriors were down Little Valley catching horses, and some more were killing beef. The place looked as if it was all alive with hostile Bannocks.

With her heart pounding, Sarah sneaked into the camp disguised in a blanket, found her father, and told him her escape plan.

"Whisper it among yourselves . . . There is no time to lose," she warned.

The women and children, pretending to search for firewood, went first. Then, under cover of darkness, Sarah and the men released some horses and slipped away.

By morning the Bannocks would be in pursuit. Sarah feared that her group, with so many on foot, would soon be overtaken. Her sister-in-law, Mattie, volunteered to ride with her to get help from the Army.

Away we started over the hills and valleys. We had to go about seventy-five miles . . . We sang and prayed to our Great Father in the Spirit-land.

Late in the afternoon of June 15, they arrived at the Sheep Ranch encampment. Sarah was so exhausted she burst into tears. In three days, she had ridden over 220 miles, a journey so remarkable that seasoned officers could scarcely believe it.

Her father would later say, "Hereafter we will look on her as our chieftain, for none of us are worthy of being chief but her."

With a heart divided, and praying for a swift end to the hostilities, Sarah valiantly served as a scout: boldly entering enemy territory alone and bringing back information that saved many lives on both sides. By midsummer the Bannock War was over.

When General Howard decorated her for bravery, stories about Sarah's exploits filled newspapers from coast to coast. New York and Chicago papers declared her a "heroic Indian woman." The "Pacific-Coast Pocahontas," an edition of the *Oregonian* proclaimed.

But what should have been Sarah's shining hour turned to darkness.

Many Paiute accused her of betrayal.

One day the commanding officer sent for me . . . I got ready and went down to the office, trembling as if something fearful was waiting for me . . . The officer said to me . . . "We are ordered to take your people to Yakima Reservation." It was just a little before Christmas.

Orders from President Rutherford B. Hayes overrode General Howard's promise of protection. For their part in the uprising, all the Paiutes—guilty or innocent—were to be punished. As a decorated Army scout, Sarah was exempt and free to live anywhere.

Instead, she chose to share the suffering of her people.

Within a week, more than five hundred Paiute were rounded up. Soldiers dragged terrified women and screaming children into pack wagons. The men thought likely to escape were shackled in chains.

The 350-mile northward trek over the towering Cascade Mountains to the Yakima Reservation—in the depth of winter—took a month.

BIA agent James H. Wilbur, a religious zealot, was as hard-hearted as Rinehart. On their arrival, the suffering Paiute were neither fed nor given warm clothing or housing.

They had a kind of shed made to put us in . . . {the} kind of shed you make
for your stock in winter time . . . Oh, how we did suffer with cold. There was no
wood, and the snow was waist-deep, and many died off just as cattle or horses do
after travelling so long in the cold.

Sarah became determined to right the wrong done to her people.

She had a little back pay owed to her by the Army. Turning once more
to General Howard, she begged him to write a letter of introduction on her
behalf to federal officials in Washington, D.C.

In January 1880, Sarah arrived in the nation's capital.

"I have come to plead for my poor people, who are dying off with broken
hearts," she told Secretary of the Interior Carl Schurz and President Hayes. She
left clutching a letter signed by Schurz that promised immediate help.

But Schurz gave in to pressure from politicians. His promise of freedom
for the Paiute was quickly broken.

For shame! for shame! You dare to cry out Liberty, when you hold us in places against our will, driving us from place to place as if we were beasts . . . Oh, for shame! You, who call yourselves the great civilization . . . I am crying out to you for justice.

After Sarah's pleas to the government failed, she turned to the public to bring attention to her people's plight—and once again took to the stage. She did not put on Wild West shows as she had so long ago as Princess Sarah. Now she appeared alone, seeking to persuade white America of the justice of her cause, through the power of her words.

For four years she toured the country, tirelessly giving speeches at churches and public meeting halls from San Francisco to Boston. The reform-minded citizens who attended her moving performances were brought to tears by her telling of the Paiute story. Her dramatic exhortations to change the reservation system had them on their feet cheering.

"It can be done," she passionately urged the crowds.

Two elderly Boston sisters were especially moved. Elizabeth Palmer Peabody and Mary Peabody Mann, widow of the famed educator Horace Mann, were influential reformers and became Sarah's close friends and stalwart supporters.

At their urging she wrote her autobiography, and with their help *Life Among the Piutes* was published in 1883.

In July of 1884, Sarah boarded a train heading west.

Her years of crusading did not end the abuses of the reservation system, but because of the public stir she had created, her people were allowed to return to their Nevada homeland. Now she was going to join them.

She still had work to do.

Her new goal was to make sure others could follow in her path.

Sarah Winnemucca at her East Coast lectures

Sarah presented a dramatic appearance when she stepped onstage in her elaborately beaded crown and dress, red leggings, and feathered necklace. The costumes that she designed and sewed were based on buckskin clothing worn by Great Plains tribes, rather than the grass garments traditionally worn by her people.

Photograph courtesy of the Granger Collection, New York

Education has done it all . . . I entreat you to take hold of this school, and give your support by sending your children . . . and when they grow up to manhood and womanhood they will bless you.

Sarah's plan was to start a school where Paiute children would be given the tools to live in the white world, while taking pride in their own culture and tradition. Elizabeth Peabody had enthusiastically pledged her support and set about fund-raising.

Getting the school established was not an easy task. Many Paiute parents viewed Sarah with suspicion because of her long association with white people, and it was known that white teachers beat their children. She spent months visiting families, begging them to send their children to her.

In June of 1885, the Peabody Institute, named for Elizabeth, opened with twenty-four pupils near the town of Lovelock on a farm run by Sarah's brother Natchez. There was no money to put up a building, so classes were held in a brush shelter. But Sarah didn't care. Nor did her pupils.

Reading, spelling, and arithmetic lessons were taught in both English and the children's native tongue. The children drew numbers in the sand and painted the words they learned on the farm fences. They did art projects using flowers and grasses that they collected in the surrounding fields and fabric scraps that Sarah got from the local ranchers. They wrote stories and put on plays based on Paiute lore. Everyone merrily joined in for songs and music-making.

Soon, Paiute parents were begging to send their children—within two years, more than four hundred students had applied for admission. Sarah's long-held dream of a school where Paiute children were loved and welcomed had come true.

The most necessary thing for the success of an Indian school
is a good interpreter, a perfect interpreter, a true interpreter . . .
I attribute the success of my school
not to my being a scholar and a good teacher
but because I am my own Interpreter
and my heart is in my work.

❖

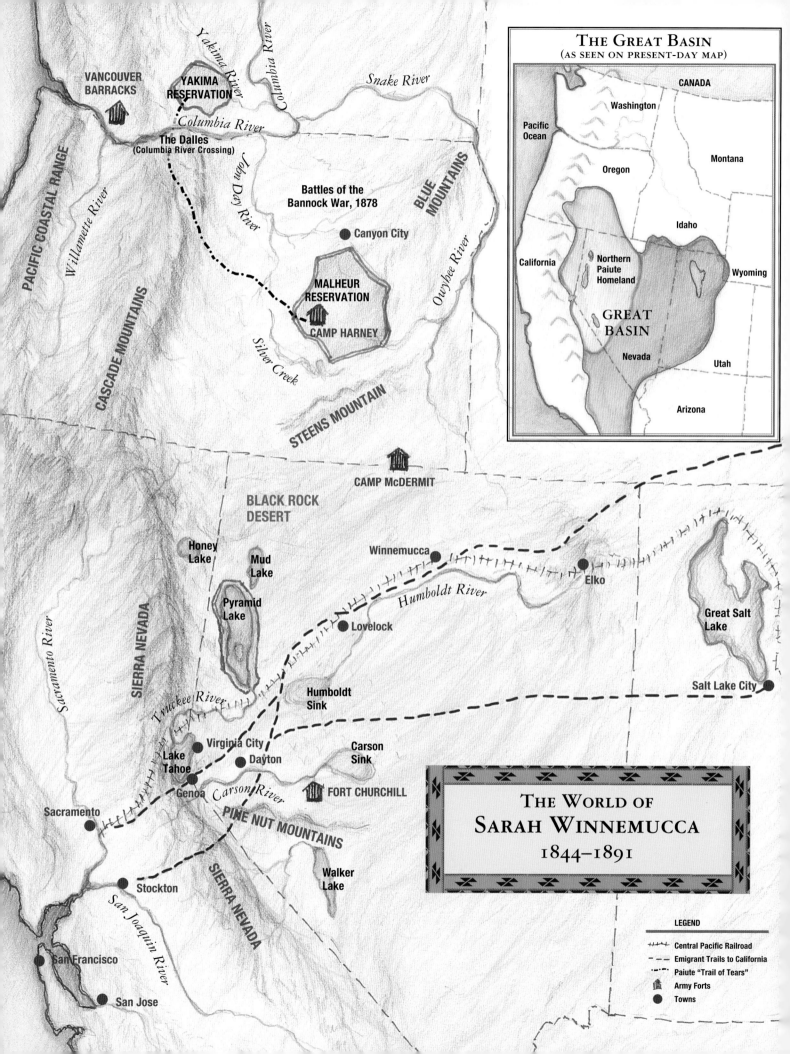

THE GREAT BASIN
(AS SEEN ON PRESENT-DAY MAP)

CANADA

Pacific Ocean

Washington

Oregon

Montana

California

Idaho

Northern Paiute Homeland

Wyoming

GREAT BASIN

Nevada

Utah

Arizona

VANCOUVER BARRACKS

Yakima River

Columbia River

Snake River

YAKIMA RESERVATION

Columbia River

The Dalles
(Columbia River Crossing)

PACIFIC COASTAL RANGE

Willamette River

John Day River

CASCADE MOUNTAINS

Battles of the Bannock War, 1878

Canyon City

BLUE MOUNTAINS

Ouyhee River

MALHEUR RESERVATION

CAMP HARNEY

Silver Creek

STEENS MOUNTAIN

CAMP McDERMIT

BLACK ROCK DESERT

Honey Lake

Mud Lake

Winnemucca

Pyramid Lake

Humboldt River

Elko

Great Salt Lake

Lovelock

Sacramento River

SIERRA NEVADA

Truckee River

Humboldt Sink

Salt Lake City

Virginia City

Lake Tahoe

Dayton

Carson Sink

Genoa

Carson River

FORT CHURCHILL

Sacramento

PINE NUT MOUNTAINS

THE WORLD OF
SARAH WINNEMUCCA
1844–1891

Stockton

SIERRA NEVADA

Walker Lake

San Francisco

San Joaquin River

San Jose

LEGEND

Central Pacific Railroad

Emigrant Trails to California

Paiute "Trail of Tears"

Army Forts

Towns

About Sarah's People

As they did with most other Native American peoples, whites bestowed a tribal name on the Northern Paiute—whose language (Uto-Aztec) is shared by the Bannocks. They are not related to the Southern Paiute tribe, whose language is very different.

In telling Sarah Winnemucca's story, I have used the contemporary spelling of Paiute. During the nineteenth century, the most common spelling was Piute, as in the title of Sarah's autobiography. Other variations were Pi-Utah and Pah-Ute. The Northern Paiute were also called Paviotso. They called themselves simply Numa, which means "people."

Before the arrival of whites, the Numa freely roamed the high desert country of the Great Basin, in what is now western Nevada, northeastern California, and southern Oregon. The tribe was made up of about two dozen loose-knit bands—each taking its name from the principal food source in the area where the band spent most of the year. Sarah Winnemucca's band, the Kuyuidika-a (Cui-ui-eaters), was named for a large black suckerfish that was abundant in Pyramid Lake. The bands gathered only for special occasions, like the spring antelope hunt and the pine nut harvest celebration in the autumn.

"Captains" were in charge of community hunts for antelope and rabbit. "Spirit doctors"—men or women believed to hold special powers—presided over ceremonies and healing. A respected male figure acted as headman, and issues were discussed in a council of elders, but the entire band took part in decision-making. The idea of a central leader did not exist—and developed only when whites demanded a single spokesperson. The word "chief" meant "talker" or "storyteller" in their language. Truckee and Winnemucca were chiefs because of their ability to persuade their people with reasoning and eloquence.

The notion of an "Indian princess" was also the creation of whites. Royal lineage did not exist in the Northern Paiute tribal structure, or in the culture of native peoples. Being the granddaughter and daughter of admired leaders gave Sarah Winnemucca status within the tribe, but her people did not call her "Princess." As a mark of respect for her accomplishments, they called her "Mother."

Women of the Numa

(*left*) Home-building was the job of the women of the Numa. Shelters needed to be quickly and easily built. Grass, tules, cattails, sagebrush, willows, and pine boughs were used for construction.

(*below*) The women wove willow baskets for all the family needs—burden baskets and winnowing trays for harvesting nuts and grains, cooking and eating baskets, water jugs, and cradleboards to carry babies.

Photographs by Edward S. Curtis, courtesy of Charles Deering McCormick Library of Special Collections, Northwestern University

SARAH IN WASHINGTON, D.C.

At all her East Coast lectures, Sarah circulated petitions seeking justice for her people and collected thousands of signatures supporting her cause. On April 22, 1884, she presented the petitions to Congress and testified before the House Committee on Indian Affairs. The outcome of her testimony was not all she hoped for, but she achieved her primary objective: permission for the Yakima prisoners to return to their homeland—without fear of arrest. The exile of the Northern Paiute was ended.

Through her association with Elizabeth Peabody, Sarah met many prominent people. Among them was Senator Henry L. Dawes of Massachusetts, who was supported by well-meaning reformers—including the influential Friends of the Indians—in his legislative proposals to solve the "Indian problem" through cultural assimilation and land grants to encourage farming.

Treaties had been broken. The reservation system, as practiced, was corrupt and inhumane. Most native peoples were living in dire poverty. To the East Coast philanthropists and church groups who sought reform, land ownership as a means to attain "civilization" and citizenship sounded like the answer.

Though Sarah initially agreed with Senator Dawes regarding farming as a tool for economic survival, she soon realized the intent of the legislation was to destroy tribal structure, and she vehemently argued against it—an opinion that put her at odds with many of her supporters.

Dawes's General Allotment Act included nearly all tribes and altered their rights without consent. The law allotted: "to each head of a family, one-quarter of a section (about 160 acres); to each single person over eighteen years of age, one-eighth of a section; to each orphan child under eighteen years of age, one-eighth of a section." The remaining tribal lands were declared "surplus" and opened up for whites to acquire for any purpose.

From its inception, the Dawes General Allotment Act of 1887 was a disaster for native peoples. Most land in the arid West was not arable—160 acres of sand could not support a family farm. Thousands of acres were returned to the government by default and then opened for white exploitation.

When the law was passed, about 150 million acres of land remained in native hands. Within twenty years, two-thirds of their land was gone.

Sarah Winnemucca's petition to the U.S. Congress

Besides release of the Yakima prisoners, Sarah's petition asked that her people be allowed to live at the now-closed Malheur Reservation. Congress refused.

Petition from Sarah Winnemucca Hopkins, and others, for land rights for Piute Indians and for the reunion of that portion of the tribe forcibly separated during the Bannock War, January 1884, HR 48A-H10.2, RG 233, Records of the U.S. House of Representatives, National Archives, Washington D.C.

SARAH'S SCHOOL: PEABODY INSTITUTE

Sarah's school—based on her own humanity and the teaching methods of Elizabeth Peabody, founder of the kindergarten movement in America, and the progressive education philosophy of Horace Mann—was revolutionary.

Sadly, the first school founded by a Native American woman was to last only four years. It fell victim to a government policy toward native people called "assimilation."

"Let all that is Indian within you die! . . . You cannot become truly American citizens, industrious, intelligent, cultured, civilized until the Indian within you is dead," a proponent said.

Agents were hired to round up children for the Indian boarding schools, like the one in Carlisle, Pennsylvania, where they were taken to be "civilized." Several times, Sarah had to prevent the kidnapping of her own students when agents tried to drag them away.

Native children were to be taught in English only—by white teachers. Curriculum was strictly limited to subjects deemed suitable to "Christianize" them. Positive mention of their heritage was not permitted. And with each passing year "Indian" education became more restrictive and punitive.

Sarah's heart was broken when the Peabody Institute closed in the summer of 1889.

In the spring of 1890, Sarah withdrew from public life and moved to Henry's Lake in Montana—an isolated wilderness area just west of what is now Yellowstone National Park—to live with her sister Elma.

Sarah Winnemucca died at the age of forty-seven on October 16, 1891.

Elizabeth Palmer Peabody (1804–94)

Elizabeth Peabody belonged to the social reform movement that developed in Boston in the mid-nineteenth century. In 1860, she introduced the kindergarten movement in America—an innovative approach to learning that used organized play, development of the senses, and involvement with nature.

Both Sarah's cause and her "model school"—as Elizabeth Peabody called it—became the embodiment of Peabody's philosophy.

Photograph courtesy of Library of Congress

United States Indian Training and Industrial School, Carlisle, Pennsylvania (1879–1918)

School life at the U.S. government's first Indian boarding school was modeled after military life. Uniforms were issued and precision drills were performed. The boys' hair was cropped—a sign of mourning in tribal culture. All the children were assigned new American names and required to speak only in English. No mention of their culture was permitted. All rules were strictly enforced. The most severe punishment for infractions was confinement in the guardhouse.

During Carlisle's existence, over 10,000 children from more than 140 tribes attended, and it served as a model for dozens of other Indian boarding schools throughout the country.

Photograph courtesy of U.S. Army Military History Institute

AUTHOR'S NOTE

Sarah Winnemucca was an extraordinary person and to this day remains a controversial figure. Strong-willed and independent-thinking—a trait that put her in constant conflict with the white power structure and sometimes with her own native people—she lived in two worlds and, sadly, was not fully accepted in either.

She was bright, vivacious, and witty, and many in white society were attracted to her charms. Two short-lived marriages were to Army officers—Edward Bartlett and Lewis Hopkins—both dashing, well-educated ne'er-do-wells. Sarah could have chosen to assimilate and spend her life within the white community, as her sister Elma did, but she treasured her culture and heritage.

Unlike many Indian rights advocates of her time, she never recommended assimilation. Her eloquent appeals to white America were for her people to be understood and treated with respect and dignity. It is for this reason that she wrote her book.

Life Among the Piutes remains an important document, as both an autobiography of a native woman and a remarkably accurate history of events—all written from memory. Books about the settlement of the West have traditionally been from the white perspective. To have Sarah Winnemucca's point of view enriches all of us.

Few Native American women are recognized for their roles in our country's history. Among them, Sarah Winnemucca is unique. Pocahontas and Sacagawea both lived in times and places where the white man was a powerless stranger in a strange land, dependent on their help for survival. Sarah, by contrast, faced a world where the fate of the native people was in the hands of the new rulers of the land.

It is to Sarah's credit that despite years of adversity she remained a peacemaker—albeit one who always spoke her mind.

In 2005, a bronze sculpture of Sarah Winnemucca was installed in the National Statuary Hall Collection at Emancipation Hall in the United States Capitol in Washington, D.C., by the State of Nevada to honor a notable person in their history.

The inscription on the pedestal reads:

SARAH WINNEMUCCA
DEFENDER OF HUMAN RIGHTS
EDUCATOR
AUTHOR OF FIRST BOOK BY A NATIVE WOMAN

Bronze sculpture of Sarah Winnemucca

By Benjamin Victor at Emancipation Hall, United States Capitol, Washington, D.C.

Photograph courtesy of Architect of the Capitol

Time Line 1844–91

1844
Sarah Winnemucca (Thocmetony) is born near Pyramid Lake.

1845–46
U.S. Army Captain John Charles Frémont arrives to explore the unmapped Great Basin. He writes, "The appearance of the country was so forbidding that I was afraid to enter it." Chief Truckee of the Northern Paiute guides him across the Sierras to California, where Frémont leads a revolt against Mexican rule. The United States declares war on Mexico on May 13, 1846.

1848
Gold is discovered at Sutter's Mill in Coloma, California, on January 24. The Mexican-American War ends on February 2 with the Treaty of Guadalupe Hidalgo, in which Mexico cedes the present-day states of California, Nevada, Utah, and parts of Arizona, Colorado, New Mexico, and Wyoming. With the inclusion of Texas (admitted as a state in 1845), the United States now controls almost all the land of southwestern America to the Pacific Ocean.

1849–50
An estimated 32,000 forty-niners cross the Great Basin on their way west to the California goldfields. Mormon Station—later known as Genoa—becomes the first town in Nevada (then Utah Territory). The Bureau of Indian Affairs becomes part of the newly created Department of the Interior and embarks on a program to move native populations onto "reserves." On September 9, 1850, California is admitted to the Union as a non-slave state.

1859–60
Silver is discovered on the east side of the Sierras. The Comstock Lode triggers a mining stampede. Native food sources are destroyed, and tension between whites and the Paiute erupts into conflict (May 12–June 2, 1860). In exchange for promises of safety from white incursion, the Paiute agree to live at Pyramid Lake—a de facto reservation (not officially recognized until 1874) administered by the BIA. Chief Truckee dies in October 1860.

1861–65
The American Civil War begins on April 12, 1861. On May 20, 1862, President Abraham Lincoln signs the Homestead Act, which makes western lands in the public domain available for settlement. Nevada is admitted to the Union on October 31, 1864. The Civil War ends on April 18, 1865.

1866–70
Westward migration into native lands increases. Violent conflicts between settlers and Indians erupt. The U.S. Army is instructed to forcibly "bring in" all "hostiles" who refuse to live on reservations.

1871
On March 3, Congress approves the Indian Appropriations Act, which ends the recognition of tribes as sovereign nations and prohibits additional treaties from being made. All natives are to be treated as individuals and legally designated "wards" of the federal government.

1879
The first students arrive at the United States Indian Training and Industrial School at Carlisle, Pennsylvania, a boarding school founded by former Indian-fighter U.S. Army Captain Richard Henry Pratt.

1880
Congress enacts regulations outlawing native religions, the practices of medicine men, festive and ritual ceremonies, and leaving the reservation without permission.

1881
Helen Hunt Jackson's book *A Century of Dishonor* is released. It details the plight of Native Americans and criticizes the U.S. government's treatment of them. It also includes Sarah Winnemucca's letter published in *Harper's Weekly* in 1870.

1887
Passage of the Dawes (or General Allotment) Act gives the president power to reduce the landholdings of the Indian nations across the country.

1891
Sarah Winnemucca dies at Henry's Lake in Montana. Her grave is unmarked. Legislation continues to be passed to reduce native landholdings. Forced assimilation and the breakup of tribal structures remain U.S. government policy until the Indian Reorganization Act of 1934.

BIBLIOGRAPHY AND RESOURCES

Direct quotations in this book are from Sarah Winnemucca's autobiography and letters—as written—and include instances of archaic spelling. Two proper names, Rinehart and Ormsby, were corrected.

I have used italics to indicate Sarah's voice. Text from *Life Among the Piutes* used as dialogue appears in quotation marks. The portion of Numaga's famous speech "Sand in the Whirlwind"—which is quoted—was originally published in *History of Nevada* in 1881.

I have also used words and phrases (in quotation marks) from newspapers of the time to give a sense of the world that Sarah faced.

Canfield, Gae Whitney. *Sarah Winnemucca of the Northern Paiutes*. Norman, Okla.: University of Oklahoma Press, 1983.

Hopkins, *Sarah Winnemucca. Life Among the Piutes: Their Wrongs and Claims*. New York: G. P. Putnam's Sons, 1883. Ed. Mrs. Horace Mann. Reprinted with a foreword by Catherine S. Fowler. Reno: University of Nevada Press, 1994.

Howard, Oliver O. "Toc-me-to-ne, an Indian Princess." *Famous Indian Chiefs I Have Known*. New York: Century, 1908.

Luchetti, Cathy, and Carol Olwell. *Women of the West*. St. George, Utah: Antelope Island Press, 1982.

Reid, John B., and Ronald M. James, eds. *Uncovering Nevada's Past: A Primary Source History of the Silver State*. Reno: University of Nevada Press, 2004.

Reno, Mona, comp. "Sarah Winnemucca, an Annotated Bibliography." Nevada State Library and Archives, 2008.

Rosinsky, Natalie M. *Sarah Winnemucca: Scout, Activist, and Teacher*. Minneapolis, Minn.: Compass Point Books, 2006.

Wheat, Margaret M. *Survival Arts of the Primitive Paiutes*. Reno: University of Nevada Press, 1967.

Zanjani, Sally. *Devils Will Reign: How Nevada Began*. Reno: University of Nevada Press, 2006.

————. *Sarah Winnemucca*. Lincoln, Neb.: University of Nebraska Press, 2001.

To find out more about Sarah Winnemucca and the time in which she lived, please visit the following Web sites:

Sarah Winnemucca, An Annotated Bibliography is available at the Nevada State Library and Archives Web site. It contains a wealth of historical information, including personal correspondence, newspaper and periodical articles, and U.S. government records. nevadaculture.org/nsla/dmdocuments/SarahWinnemucca_bibliography2008.pdf

The Carlisle Indian Industrial School Research Pages Web site (maintained by Barbara Landis) has a history of the school and personal stories of those who attended. home.epix.net/~landis/

*In memory of
Naomi Tumarkin*

Copyright © 2012 by Deborah Kogan Ray
All rights reserved
Distributed in Canada by
D&M Publishers, Inc.
Color separations by KHL Chroma Graphics
Printed in China by
Toppan Leefung Printing Ltd.,
Dongguan City, Guangdong Province
Designed by Barbara Grzeslo
First edition, 2012
1 3 5 7 9 10 8 6 4 2

mackids.com

Library of Congress Cataloging-in-Publication Data
Ray, Deborah Kogan, 1940–
    Paiute princess : the story of Sarah Winnemucca / Deborah Kogan Ray. — 1st ed.
        p. cm.
    Includes bibliographical references.
    ISBN: 978-0-374-39897-2
    1. Hopkins, Sarah Winnemucca, 1844?–1891—Juvenile literature. 2. Paiute women—Biography—Juvenile literature. 3. Paiute Indians—Biography—Juvenile literature. 4. Women political activists—West (U.S.)—Biography—Juvenile literature. 5. Indians of North America—Civil rights—History—19th century—Juvenile literature. 6. American literature—Indian authors—Biography—Juvenile literature. I. Title.

E99.P2R39 2011
979.004'9745769—dc22
{B}
                                            2009046090